3rd Grade Science Life Sciences in Eco Systems

Textbook Edition

Speedy Publishing LLC
40 E. Main St. #1156
Newark, DE 19711
www.speedypublishing.com

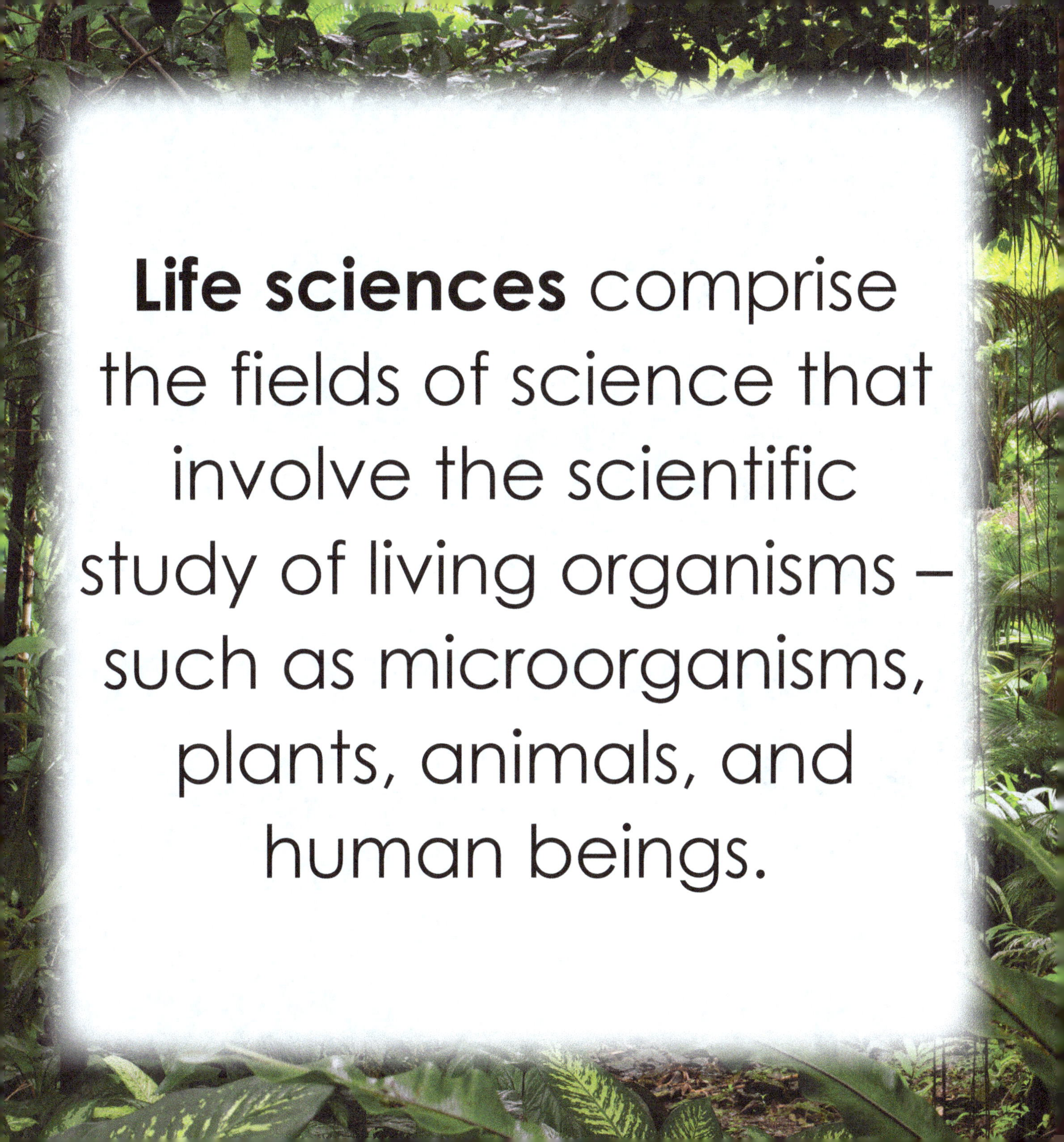

Life sciences comprise the fields of science that involve the scientific study of living organisms – such as microorganisms, plants, animals, and human beings.

Biology is the branch of natural science concerned with the study of life and living organisms, including their structure, function, growth, evolution, distribution, and taxonomy.

Agriculture is the study of producing crops and raising livestock, with an emphasis on practical applications.

My Body

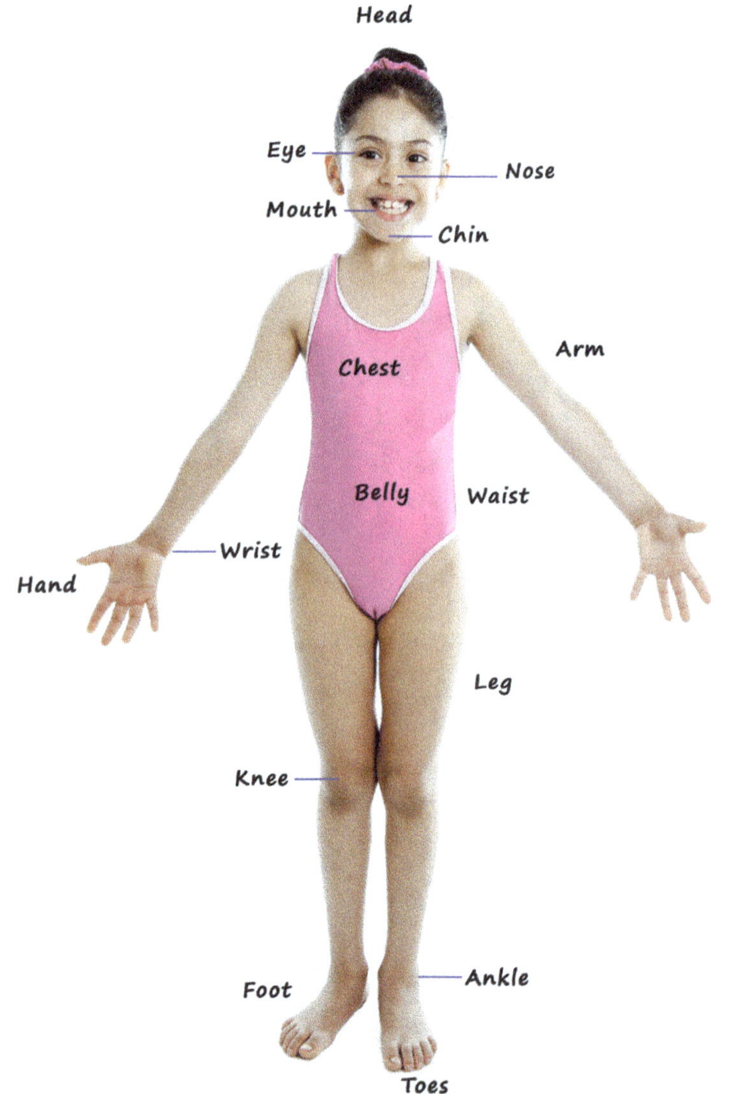

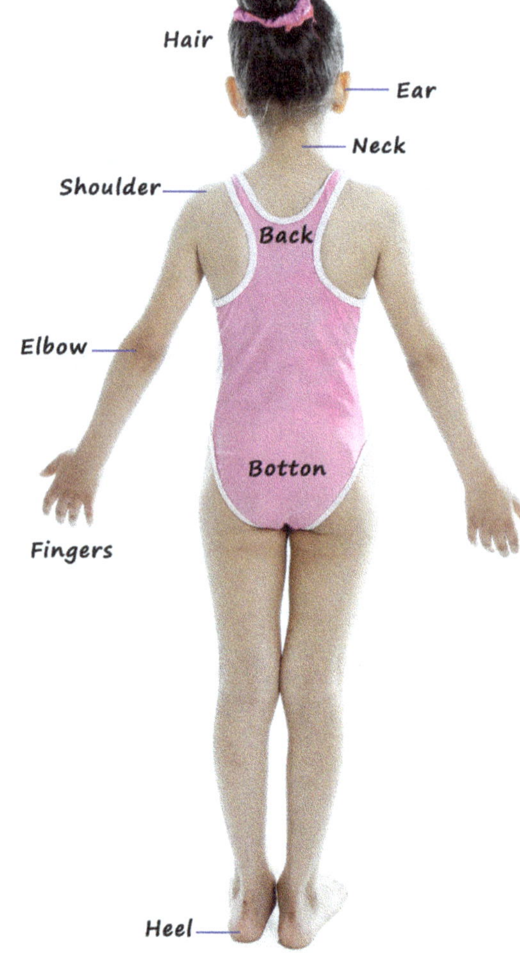

Front

Back

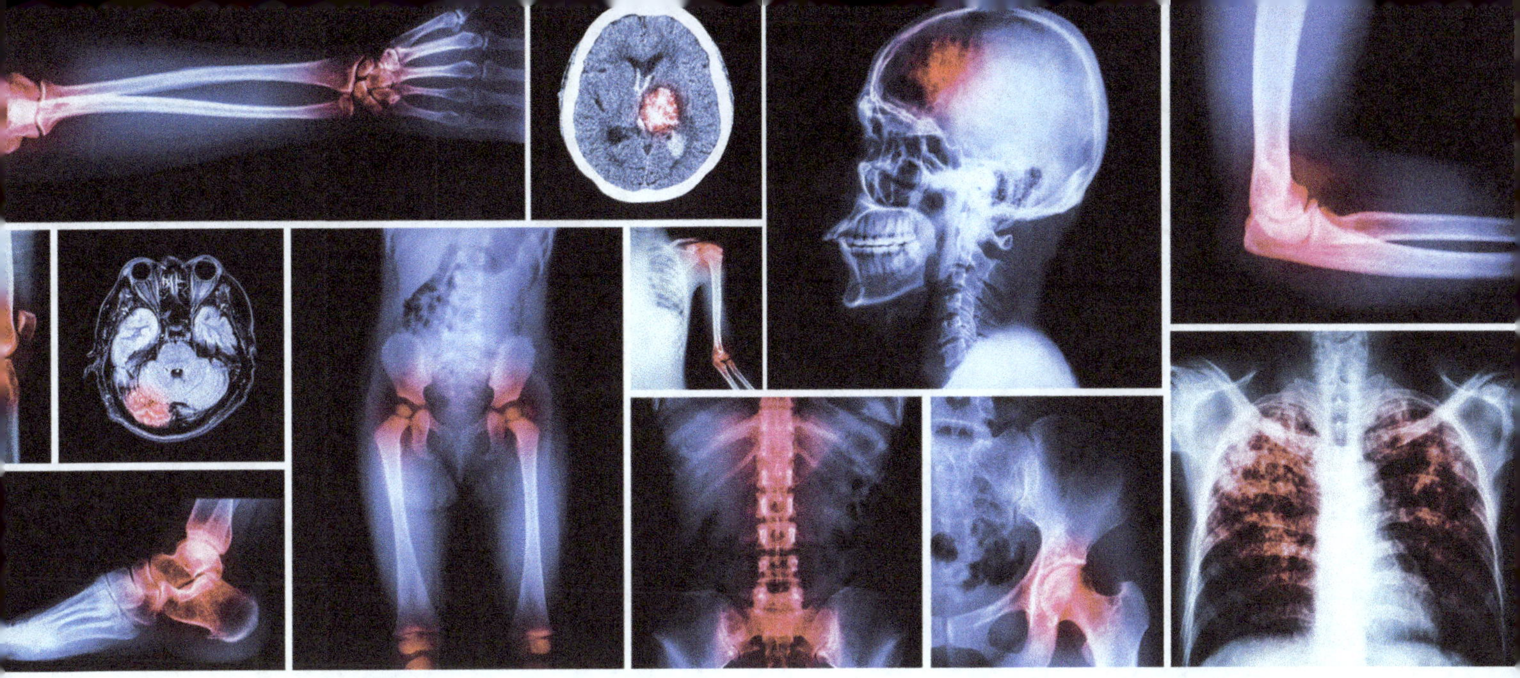

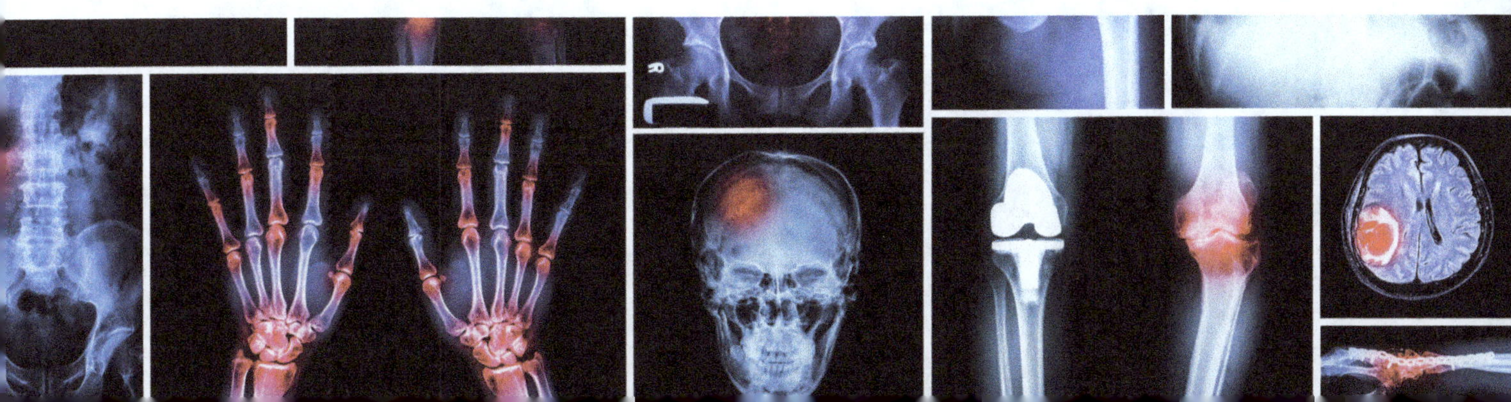

Anatomy is the study of form and function, in plants, animals, and other organisms, or specifically in humans.

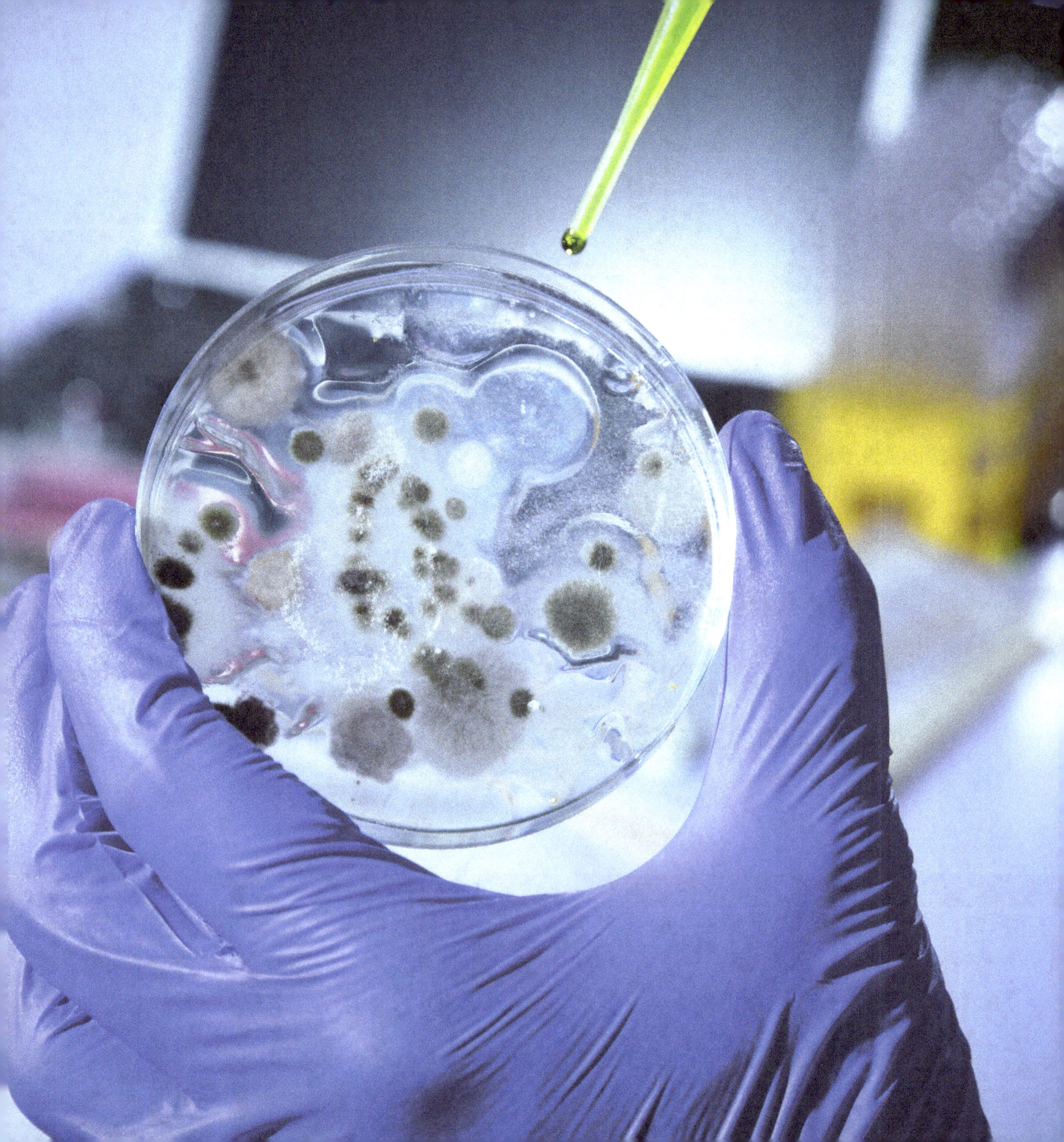

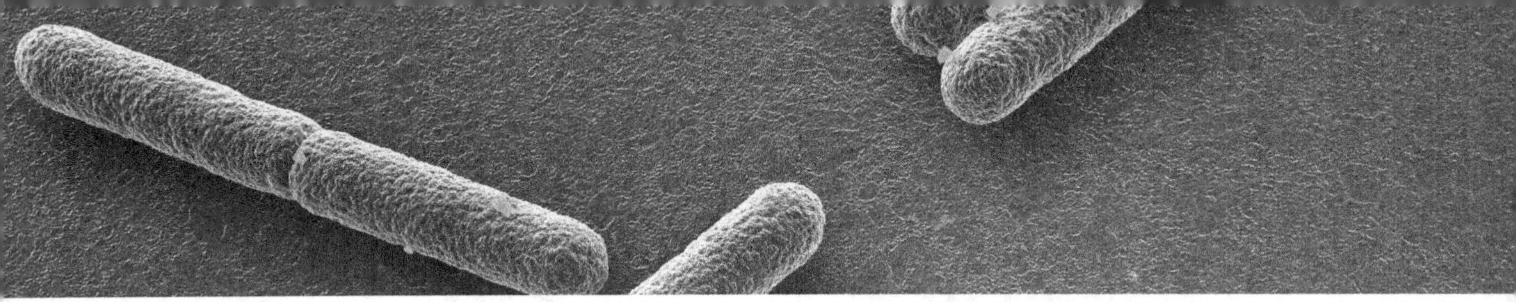

Bacteriology is the study of bacteria.

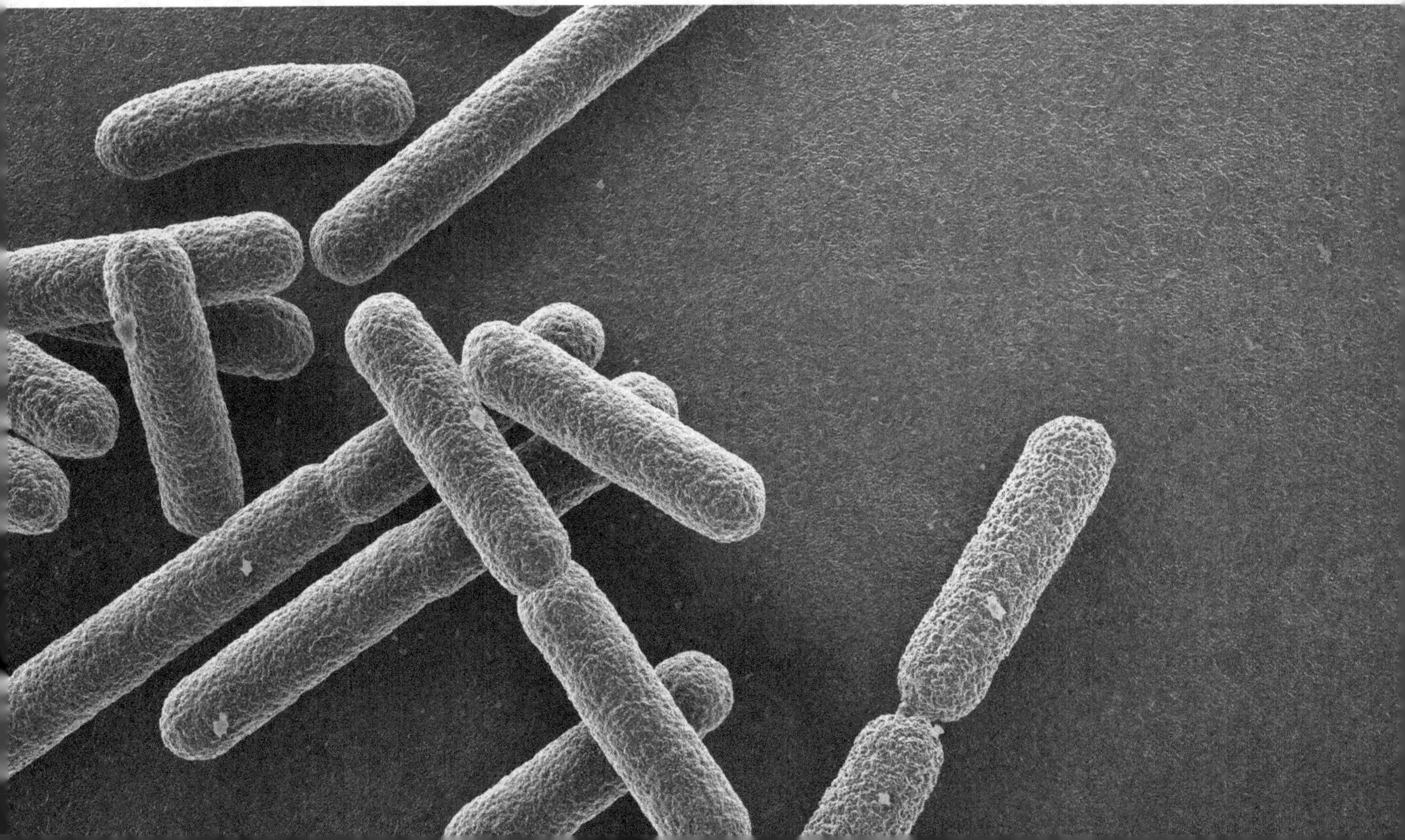

Botany is the study of plants.

Ecology is the study of the interactions of living organisms with one another and with the non-living elements of their environment.

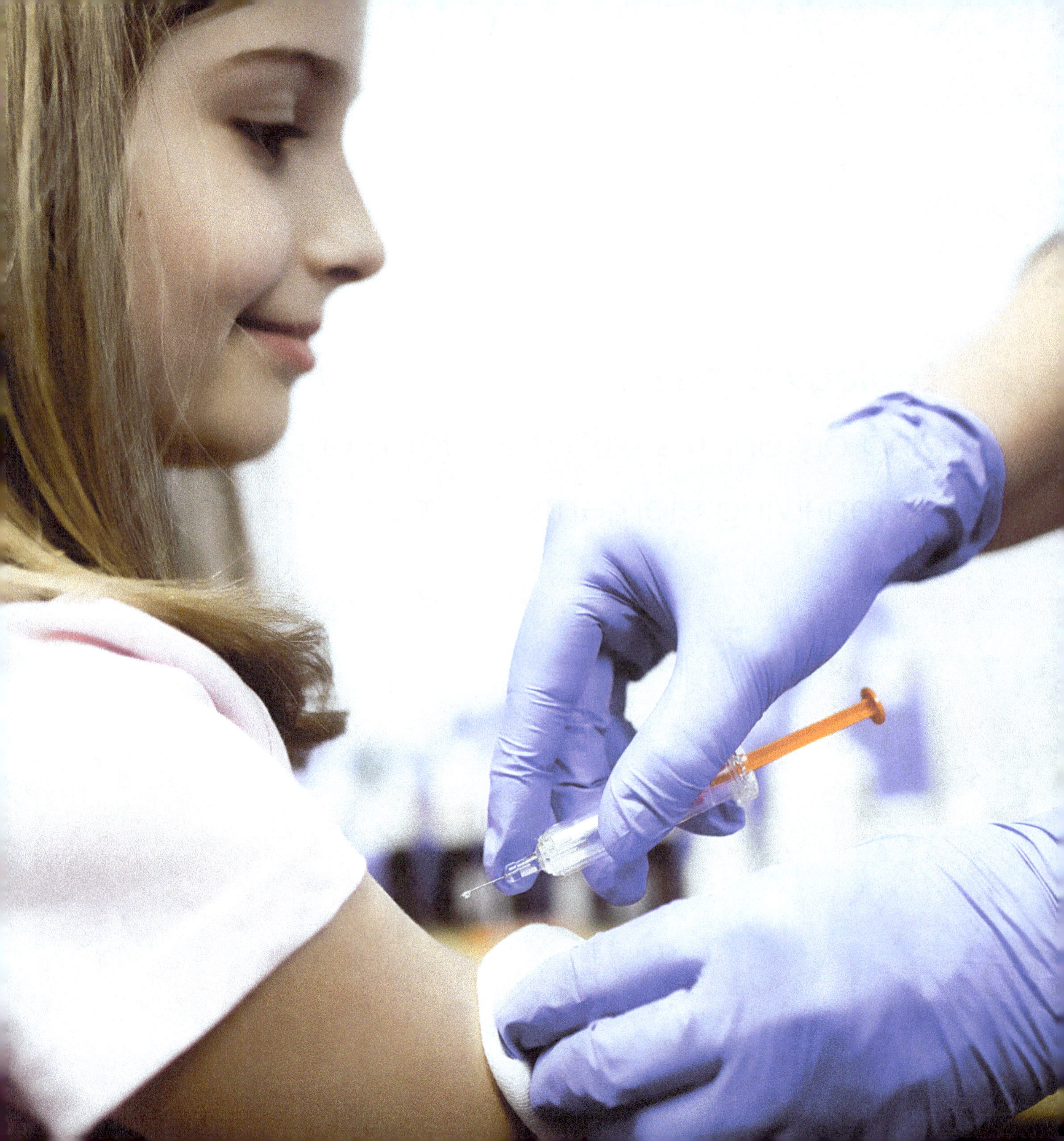

Epidemiology is the a major component of public health research, studying factors affecting the health of populations.

Genetics is the study of genes and heredity.

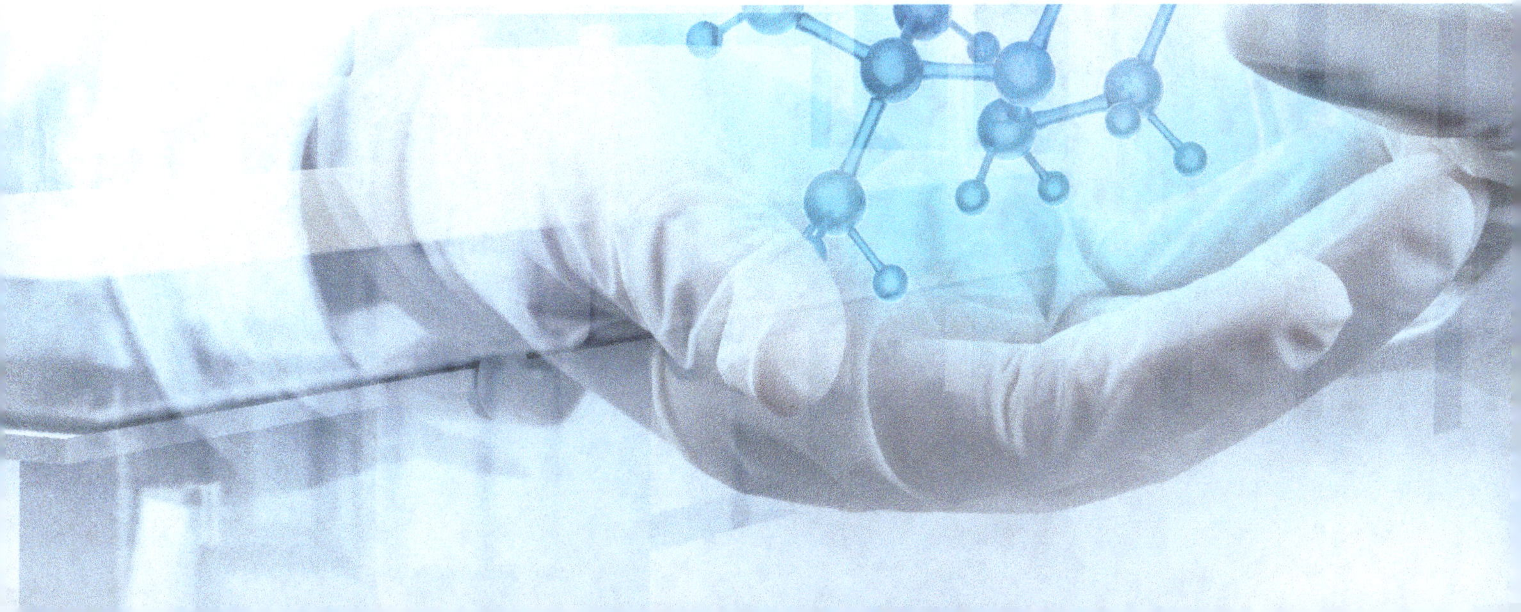

3.0
mL
2015-03
LOT
5.4mg
STERILE R
2015-03
3.0
mL
45.8
89.0
29.1
33.2
13.1
309
89.8
31.6
33.2
12.8
355
10:18
215
155
10 23

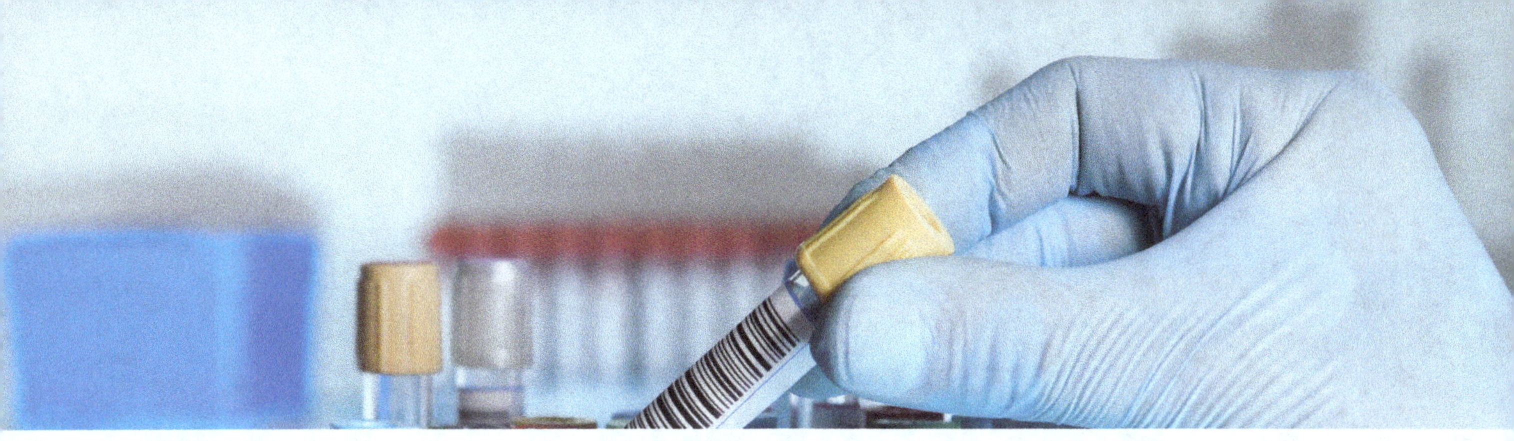

Hematology (also known as Haematology) is the study of blood and blood-forming organs.

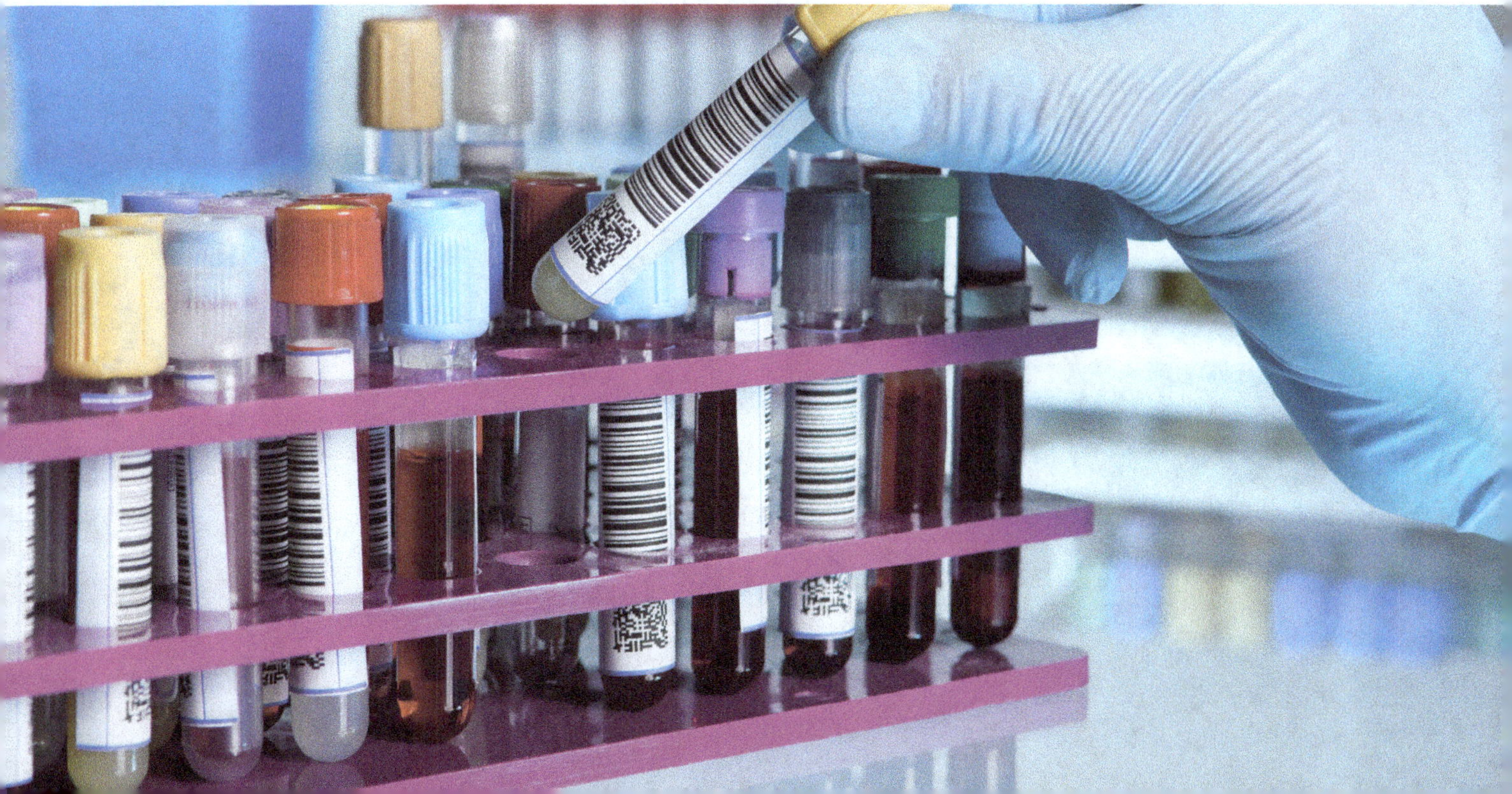

Marine biology (or Biological oceanography) is the study of ocean ecosystems, plants, animals, and other living beings.

Microbiology is the study of microscopic organisms (microorganisms) and their interactions with other living things.

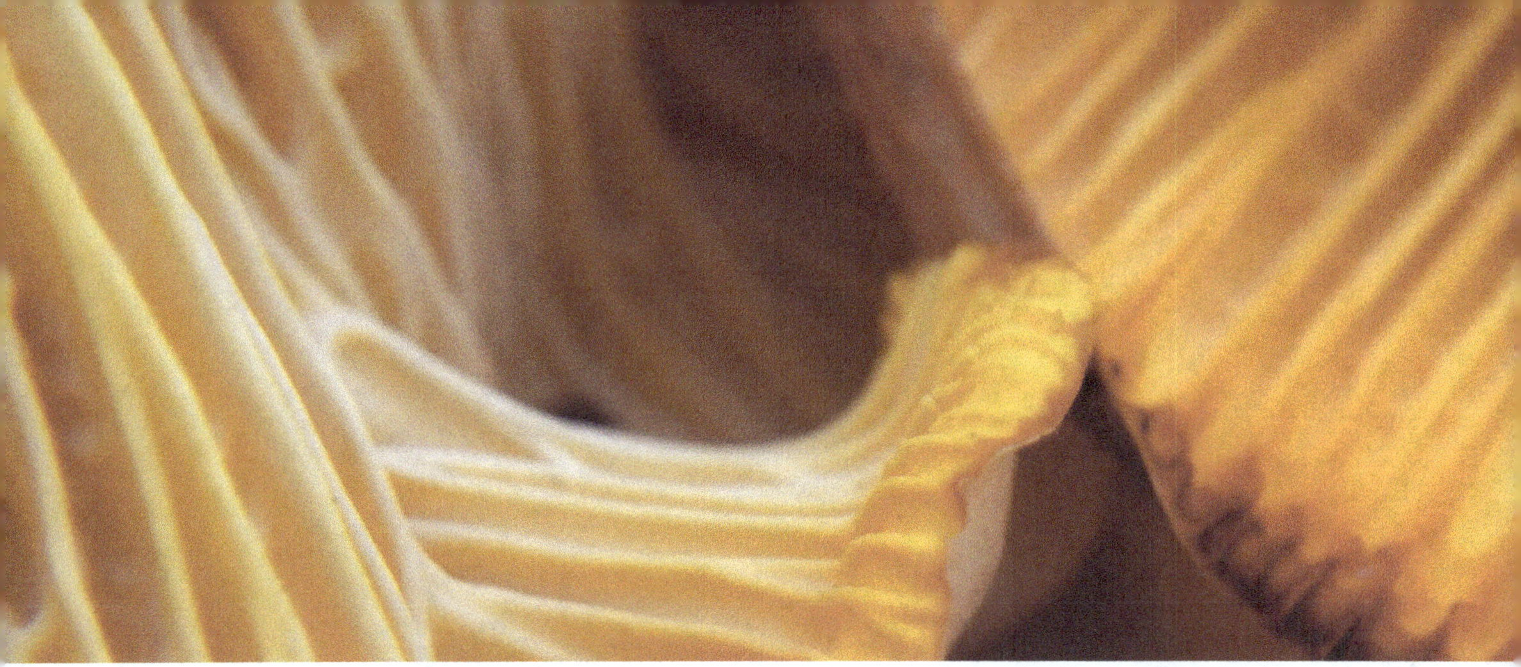

Mycology is the study of fungi.

Oceanography is the study of the ocean, including ocean life, environment, geography, weather, and other aspects influencing the ocean.

Paleontology is the study of fossils
and sometimes geographic
evidence of prehistoric life.

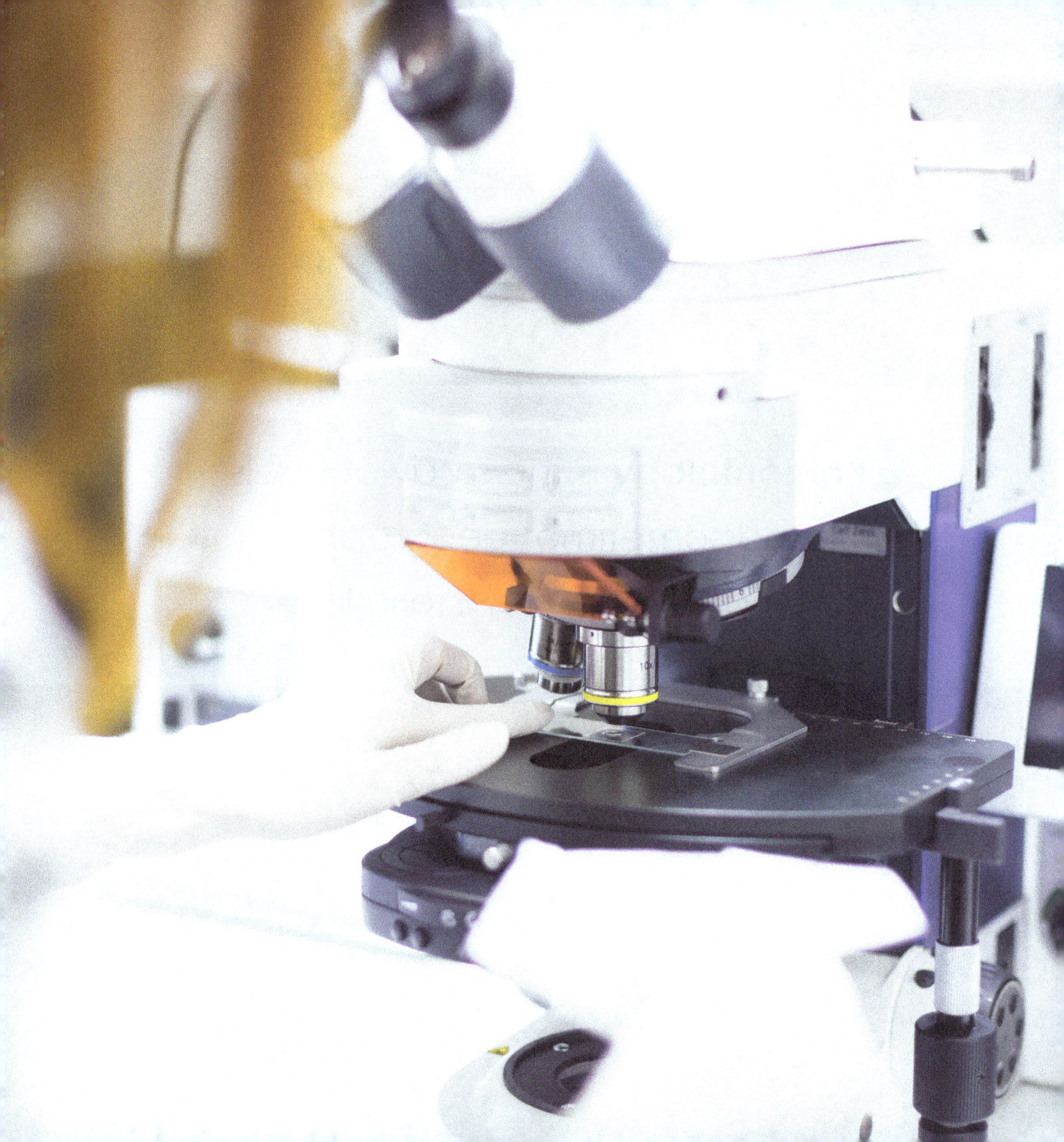

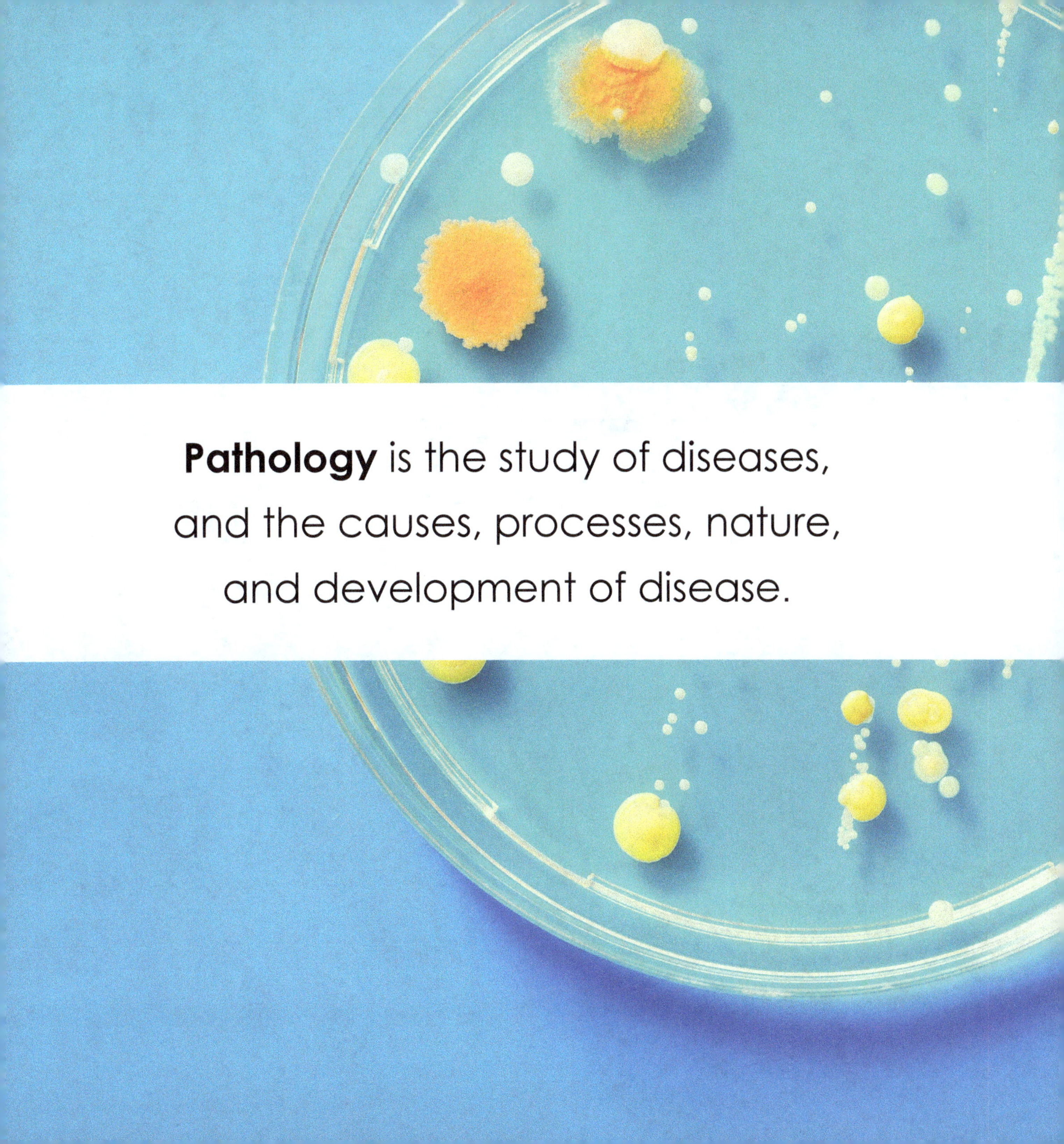

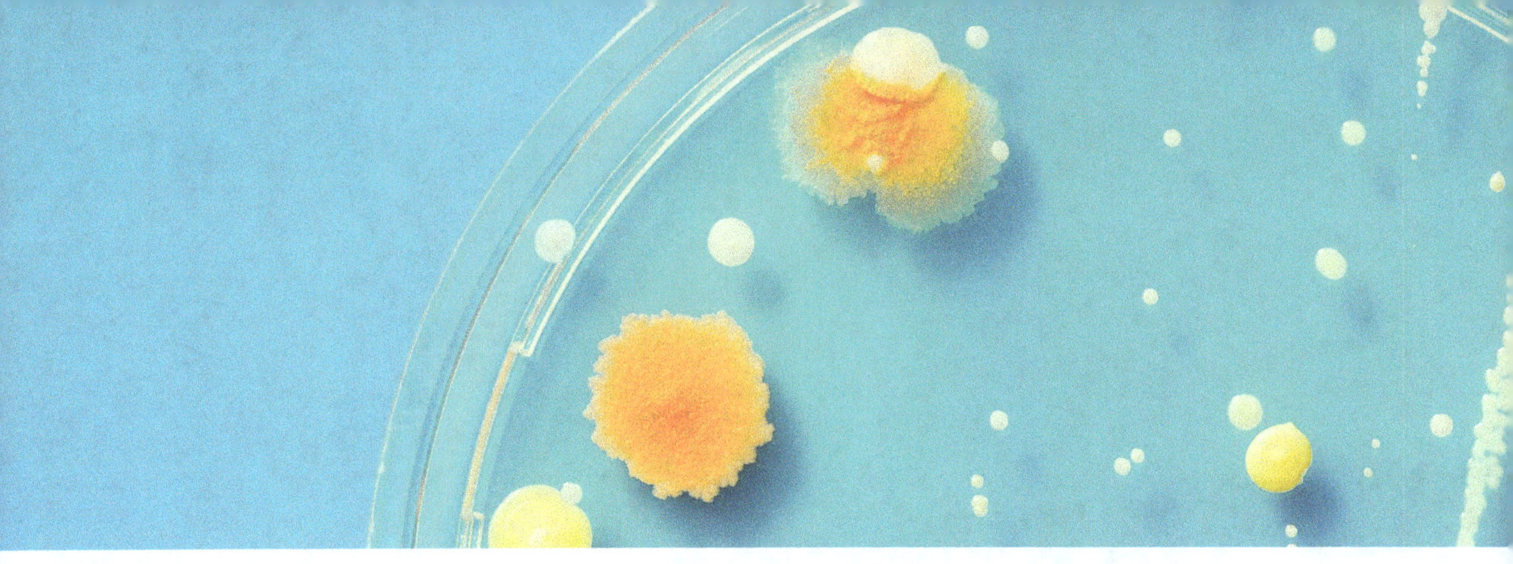

Pathology is the study of diseases, and the causes, processes, nature, and development of disease.

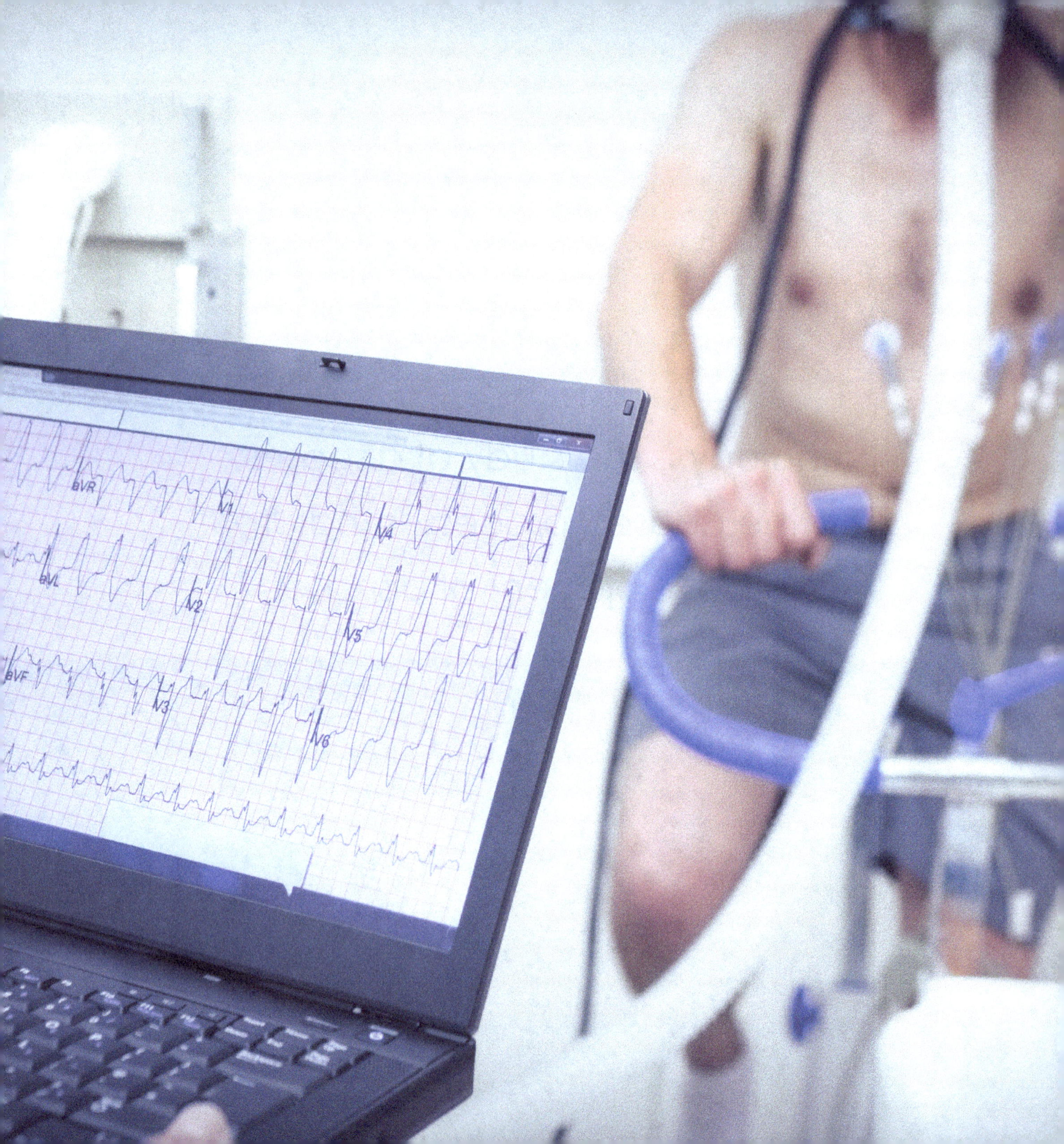
aVR
aVL
aVF
V1
V2
V3
V4
V5
V6

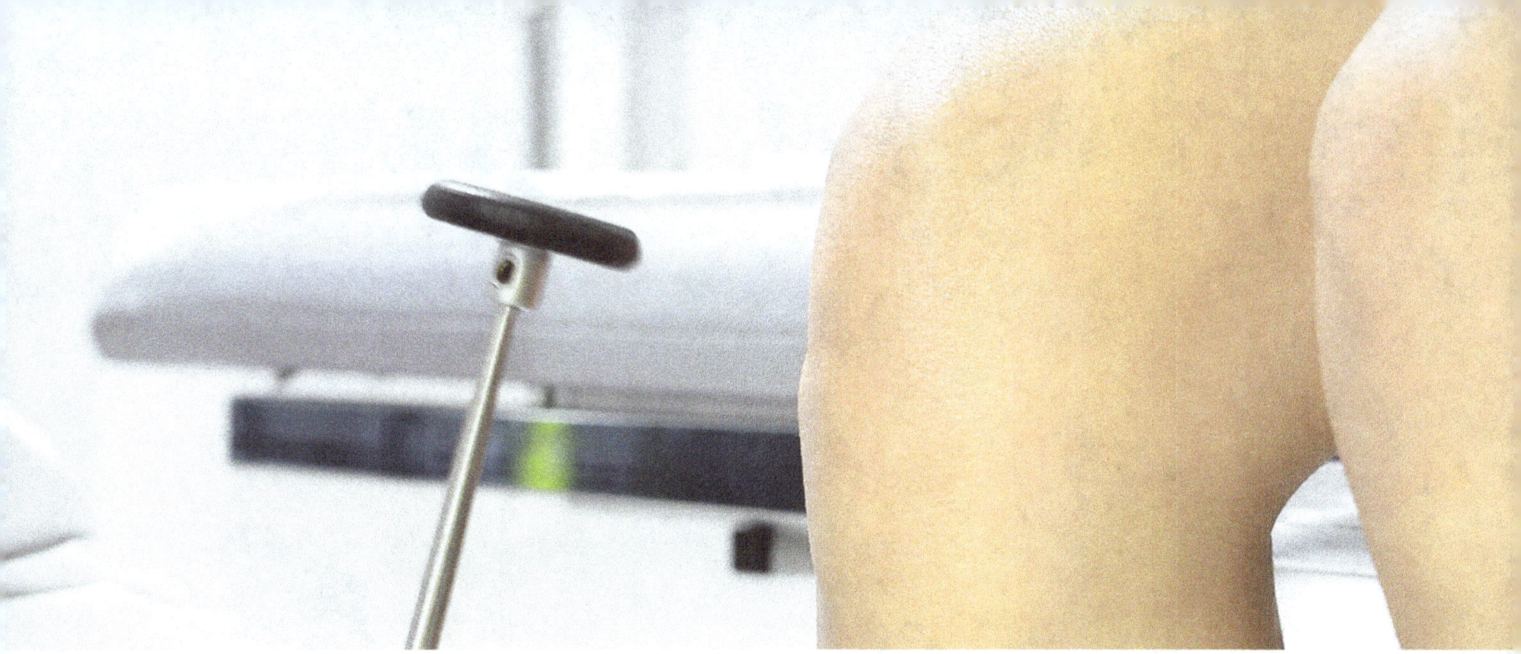

Physiology is the study of the functioning
of living organisms and the organs
and parts of living organisms.

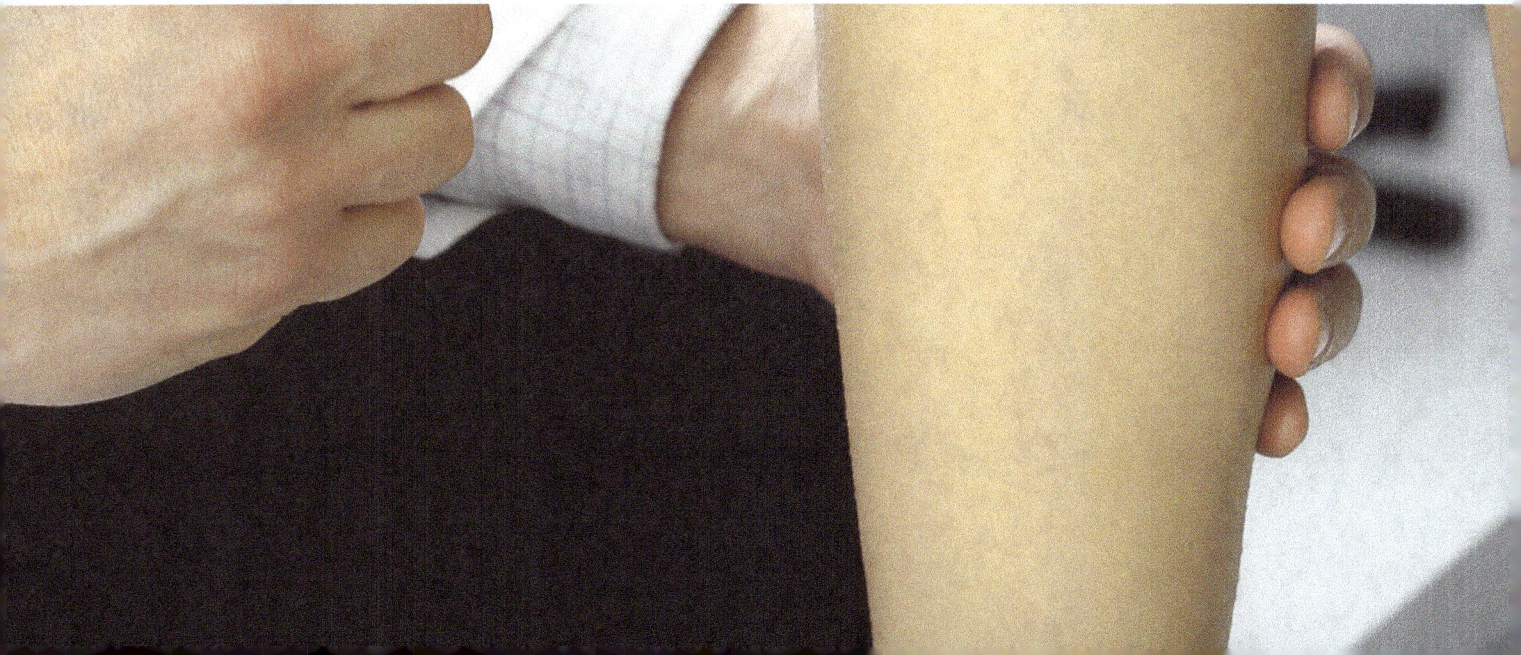

Toxicology is the study of the effects
of chemicals on living organisms.

Zoology is the study of animals, including classification, physiology, development, and behavior.

Visit
BABY PROFESSOR
EDUCATION KIDS
www.BabyProfessorBooks.com
to download Free Baby Professor eBooks
and view our catalog of new and exciting
Children's Books